This Book Belongs To

Name: _____

Address: _____

_____

Email: _____

Phone: _____

One Thing Devotional Journal

Powered by

stikwidit.com

Follow Us

How to Use this Devotional Journal

This journal is meant to be a companion to your devotional time with God. Whether your routine is to read a daily devotional book, or follow a Reading Plan on YouVersion or watch a sermon/spiritual message or just read the bible. The journal is here to help with <u>Consistency</u>, <u>Depth</u>, <u>Structure</u> and <u>Growth</u>. Documenting your prayers & thoughts as you navigate life and God's Word is a great way to stimulate and maintain good spiritual health.

So grab your journal, pen, Bible (on the phone if you must) then choose a time and place and let's all be very intentional about knowing God and loving him with every cell in our bodies.

Be sure to allow for times of being still in His presence and receiving His love. He created you to love you! Embrace this truth as you ponder, document and wrestle with God.

P.S. Feel free to be candid in your written thoughts and be sure to store the journal in a private place.

P.P.S. Have you ever been in a situation where you said you would pray for someone and forgot? I personally love this journal because now I write it down and not forget :)

My Words to God

Date:_____

Gratitude & Praise

"Enter his gates with thanksgiving and his courts with praise...". Jesus did not complain that He had no food to feed 5000 people. With gratitude He gave thanks and God made a way! List the things that fills you with gratitude. 🙌

Prayer for Others

Love for God is manifested in love for others. Show love for others by praying for them. Practice putting others needs before your own. So that like John the Baptist, you will decrease and Christ will increase in you. This helps to reduce your selfishness and increase your Christlikeness.

Prayers for Self

"Give us today our daily bread...And lead us not into temptation, but deliver us from the evil one." Mat. 6: 11&13 Pray for your personal righteousness - that all your thoughts, and resulting actions, will obey Christ. Pray for your needs and wants. Let God know what's on your heart.

God's Word to Me

Reflections from Bible Time/Devotions

"I have hidden your word in my heart that I might not sin against you..." - Use this section to help with meditating on God's Word. Writing helps you to remember and internalize God's message. Answer questions like: What did I learn? How does this passage apply to my life?

Memory Verse

Feel free to choose a new verse each day, or week or month. Here is a good one to start you off: **Psalms 119:105** "Your word is a lamp for my feet, a light on my path."

Impressions

Take a moment to listen to the Holy Spirit and jot down anything He may be speaking to your heart. It could be: forgive John, help Jo, listen more to your spouse or kid. Or write down answered prayers.

"When we work, we work. When we pray, God works."
- James Hudson Taylor

My Words to God

Date:_____

Gratitude & Praise

Prayer for Others

Prayers for Self

God's Word to Me

Reflections from Bible Time/Devotions

_____

_____

_____

_____

_____

Memory Verse

_____

_____

_____

Impressions

_____

_____

_____

_____

"You are the only Bible some unbelievers will ever read."
- John MacArthur

My Words to God

Date:_____

Gratitude & Praise

What blessings have I received today?

Prayer for Others

List the people I care for

Prayers for Self

What personal needs or desires do I want to express?
Tell God what is on your heart & mind

God's Word to Me

Reflections from Bible Time/Devotions

Memory Verse

Impressions

"We have to pray with our eyes on God, not on the difficulties."
- Oswald Chambers

My Words to God

Date:_____

Gratitude & Praise

What filled your heart with gratitude / praise?

_____

_____

_____

_____

Prayer for Others

Who is in need of prayer today?

_____

_____

_____

_____

Prayers for Self

Let your mind wander and write it all for God to answer. What's on your heart? Let it rest.

_____

_____

_____

_____

God's Word to Me

<u>Reflections from Bible Time/Devotions</u>

<u>Memory Verse</u>

<u>Impressions</u>

"Let no debt remain outstanding, except the continuing debt to love one another, for whoever loves others has fulfilled the law"
- Romans 13:8

My Words to God

Date:_____

Gratitude & Praise

Prayer for Others

Prayers for Self

God's Word to Me

Reflections from Bible Time/Devotions

....

....

....

....

....

Memory Verse

....

....

....

Impressions

....

....

....

....

"To judge a person's heart is only to expose what's in your own"
- Frank Viola

My Words to God

Date:_____

Gratitude & Praise

Prayer for Others

Prayers for Self

God's Word to Me

Reflections from Bible Time/Devotions

Memory Verse

Impressions

"A man ought to live so that everybody knows he is a
Christian... and most of all, his family ought to know"
- D.L. Moody

My Words to God

Date:_____

Gratitude & Praise

Prayer for Others

Prayers for Self

God's Word to Me

Reflections from Bible Time/Devotions

....

....

....

....

....

Memory Verse

....

....

....

Impressions

....

....

....

....

"He became what we are that He might make us what He is"
- St. Athanasius

My Words to God

Date:_____

Gratitude & Praise

_____
_____
_____
_____

Prayer for Others

_____
_____
_____
_____

Prayers for Self

_____
_____
_____
_____

God's Word to Me

Reflections from Bible Time/Devotions

....

....

....

....

....

Memory Verse

....

....

....

Impressions

....

....

....

....

"Prayer is not so much an act as it is an attitude – an attitude
of dependency, dependency upon God"
- A.W. Pink

My Words to God

Date:_____

Gratitude & Praise

Prayer for Others

Prayers for Self

God's Word to Me

Reflections from Bible Time/Devotions

Memory Verse

Impressions

"Nothing so clearly discovers a spiritual man as his treatment
of an erring brother"
- St. Augustine

My Words to God

Date:_____

Gratitude & Praise

What filled your heart with gratitude / praise?

Prayer for Others

List those in need please

Prayers for Self

Let us recognize our deep longing. Father, I'm asking forgiveness.
God that I will be strengthened to mind

God's Word to Me

Reflections from Bible Time/Devotions

_____
_____
_____
_____
_____

Memory Verse

_____
_____
_____

Impressions

_____
_____
_____

"God cannot give us a happiness and peace apart from
Himself, because it is not there. There is no such thing"
- C.S. Lewis

My Words to God

Date:_____

Gratitude & Praise

_____

_____

_____

_____

Prayer for Others

_____

_____

_____

_____

Prayers for Self

_____

_____

_____

_____

God's Word to Me

Reflections from Bible Time/Devotions

....

....

....

....

....

Memory Verse

....

....

....

Impressions

....

....

....

"If Jesus Christ be God and died for me, then no sacrifice can
be too great for me to make for Him"
- C.T. Studd

My Words to God

Date:_____

Gratitude & Praise

Prayer for Others

Prayers for Self

God's Word to Me

Reflections from Bible Time/Devotions

Memory Verse

Impressions

"Character may be manifested in the great moments, but it is
made in the small ones"
- Phillips Brooks

My Words to God

Date:_____

Gratitude & Praise

Prayer for Others

Prayers for Self

God's Word to Me

Reflections from Bible Time/Devotions

....

....

....

....

....

Memory Verse

....

....

....

Impressions

....

....

....

....

"Maturity in the Christian life is measured by only one test:
how much closer to His character have we become?"
- Elyse Fitzpatrick

My Words to God

Date:_____

Gratitude & Praise

What filled your heart with reasons to be grateful?

Prayer for Others

Who needs your help today?

Prayers for Self

Let your prayer show honest sadness for sinful ways.
Tell God what your request is today.

God's Word to Me

Reflections from Bible Time/Devotions

....

....

....

....

....

Memory Verse

....

....

....

Impressions

....

....

....

"Our love grows soft if it is not strengthened by truth, and
our truth grows hard if it is not softened by love"
- John Stott

My Words to God

Date:_____

Gratitude & Praise

···

···

···

···

Prayer for Others

···

···

···

···

Prayers for Self

···

···

···

···

···

God's Word to Me

Reflections from Bible Time/Devotions

Memory Verse

Impressions

"Faith never knows where it is being led, but it loves and knows the One who is leading"
- Oswald Chambers

My Words to God

Date:_____

Gratitude & Praise

....

....

....

....

Prayer for Others

....

....

....

....

Prayers for Self

....

....

....

....

God's Word to Me

Reflections from Bible Time/Devotions

Memory Verse

Impressions

"God calls us to go against the grain when the grain is going against God. Be IN the world, not OF the world."
- Tony Evans

My Words to God

Date:_____

Gratitude & Praise

Prayer for Others

Prayers for Self

God's Word to Me

Reflections from Bible Time/Devotions

Memory Verse

Impressions

"It is the duty of every Christian to be Christ to his neighbor"
- Martin Luther

My Words to God

Date:_____

Gratitude & Praise

_____

_____

_____

_____

Prayer for Others

_____

_____

_____

_____

Prayers for Self

_____

_____

_____

_____

God's Word to Me

Reflections from Bible Time/Devotions

Memory Verse

Impressions

"It is no use walking anywhere to preach unless our walking is our preaching"
- Francis of Assisi

My Words to God

Date:_____

Gratitude & Praise

....

....

....

....

Prayer for Others

....

....

....

....

Prayers for Self

....

....

....

....

God's Word to Me

Reflections from Bible Time/Devotions

....

....

....

....

Memory Verse

....

....

....

Impressions

....

....

....

"If the Holy Spirit guides us, He will do it according to the
Scriptures and never contrary to them"
- George Muller

My Words to God

Date:_____

Gratitude & Praise

What filled your heart with gratitude & praise?

Prayer for Others

List those you want to pray for...

Prayers for Self

Let God in - open to open & listen. Invite Him to be near
Tell God what's on your heart & mind

God's Word to Me

Reflections from Bible Time/Devotions

....

....

....

....

....

Memory Verse

....

....

....

Impressions

....

....

....

....

"God uses men who are weak and feeble enough to lean on
Him"
- Hudson Taylor

My Words to God

Date:_____

Gratitude & Praise

Prayer for Others

Prayers for Self

God's Word to Me

Reflections from Bible Time/Devotions

....

....

....

....

....

Memory Verse

....

....

....

Impressions

....

....

....

....

"Humble yourselves, therefore, under God's mighty hand, that he may lift you up
in due time. Cast all your anxiety on him because he cares for you"
-1 Peter 5:6-7

My Words to God

Date:_____

Gratitude & Praise

....

....

....

....

Prayer for Others

....

....

....

....

Prayers for Self

....

....

....

....

God's Word to Me

Reflections from Bible Time/Devotions

Memory Verse

Impressions

"To add value to others, one must first value others"
- John Maxwell

My Words to God

Date:_____

Gratitude & Praise

What filled your heart with gratitude & praise?

Prayer for Others

List the people God's people:

Prayers for Self

Let your requests show the open & thirst for righteousness
& God's will act on your heart & mind

God's Word to Me

Reflections from Bible Time/Devotions

....

....

....

....

....

Memory Verse

....

....

....

Impressions

....

....

....

....

"Dear Jesus...how foolish of me to have called for human help when You are here"
- Corrie ten Boom

My Words to God

Date:_____

Gratitude & Praise

_____

_____

_____

_____

Prayer for Others

_____

_____

_____

_____

Prayers for Self

_____

_____

_____

_____

God's Word to Me

Reflections from Bible Time/Devotions

Memory Verse

Impressions

"It is not the strength of your faith but the object of your
faith that actually saves you"
- Timothy Keller

My Words to God

Date:_____

Gratitude & Praise

....

....

....

....

Prayer for Others

....

....

....

....

Prayers for Self

....

....

....

....

God's Word to Me

Reflections from Bible Time/Devotions

Memory Verse

Impressions

"Let your faith be bigger than your fears"
- Hebrews 13:6

My Words to God

Date:_____

Gratitude & Praise

What filled your heart with gratitude & praise?

....

....

....

....

Prayer for Others

Lift the people and needs

....

....

....

....

Prayers for Self

Let your prayers show hunger & thirst for righteousness

Tell God what you really are afraid of

....

....

....

....

God's Word to Me

Reflections from Bible Time/Devotions

Memory Verse

Impressions

"The great thing to remember is that though our feelings
come and go God's love for us does not."
- C.S. Lewis

My Words to God

Date:_____

Gratitude & Praise

_____

_____

_____

_____

Prayer for Others

_____

_____

_____

_____

Prayers for Self

_____

_____

_____

_____

God's Word to Me

Reflections from Bible Time/Devotions

Memory Verse

Impressions

"God put us here on this carnival ride. We close our eyes,
never knowing where it'll take us next"
- Carrie Underwood

My Words to God

Date:_____

Gratitude & Praise

_____

_____

_____

Prayer for Others

_____

_____

_____

_____

Prayers for Self

_____

_____

_____

_____

God's Word to Me

Reflections from Bible Time/Devotions

Memory Verse

Impressions

> "Life with God is not immunity from difficulties, but peace
> in difficulties."
> - C.S. Lewis

My Words to God

Date:_____

Gratitude & Praise

....

....

....

....

Prayer for Others

....

....

....

....

Prayers for Self

....

....

....

....

....

God's Word to Me

Reflections from Bible Time/Devotions

_____

_____

_____

_____

Memory Verse

_____

_____

_____

Impressions

_____

_____

_____

"Forgive and give as if it were your last opportunity. Love like
there's no tomorrow, and if tomorrow comes, love again"
- Max Lucado

My Words to God

Date:_____

Gratitude & Praise

Prayer for Others

Prayers for Self

God's Word to Me

Reflections from Bible Time/Devotions

....

....

....

....

....

....

Memory Verse

....

....

....

Impressions

....

....

....

....

"Character can not be developed in ease and quiet. Only through experience of trial and suffering can the soul be strengthened, ambition inspired, and success achieved"
- Helen Keller

My Words to God

Date:_____

Gratitude & Praise

_____

_____

_____

_____

Prayer for Others

_____

_____

_____

_____

Prayers for Self

_____

_____

_____

_____

God's Word to Me

Reflections from Bible Time/Devotions

....

....

....

....

Memory Verse

....

....

....

Impressions

....

....

....

"To walk the spiritual path is to continually step out into the unknown"
- Wallace Huey

My Words to God

Date:_____

Gratitude & Praise

Prayer for Others

Prayers for Self

God's Word to Me

Reflections from Bible Time/Devotions

Memory Verse

Impressions

"There's a lot that is good in your life–don't take it for granted. Don't
get so focused on the struggles that you miss the gift of today"
- Joel Osteen

My Words to God

Date:_____

Gratitude & Praise

_____

_____

_____

_____

Prayer for Others

_____

_____

_____

_____

Prayers for Self

_____

_____

_____

_____

God's Word to Me

Reflections from Bible Time/Devotions

Memory Verse

Impressions

"Something revolutionary happens in the heart when you recognize that every single person you will ever meet is made in the image of God"
- Jackie Hill Perry

My Words to God

Date:_____

Gratitude & Praise

....

....

....

....

Prayer for Others

....

....

....

....

Prayers for Self

....

....

....

....

God's Word to Me

Reflections from Bible Time/Devotions

....
....
....
....
....

Memory Verse

....
....
....

Impressions

....
....
....
....

"Partial obedience is really only disobedience made to look acceptable"
- Bill Arnold

My Words to God

Date:_____

Gratitude & Praise

_____
_____
_____
_____

Prayer for Others

_____
_____
_____
_____

Prayers for Self

_____
_____
_____
_____
_____

God's Word to Me

Reflections from Bible Time/Devotions

Memory Verse

Impressions

"God soon turns from His wrath, but he never turns from his love."
- C.H. Spurgeon

My Words to God

Date:_____

Gratitude & Praise

Prayer for Others

Prayers for Self

God's Word to Me

Reflections from Bible Time/Devotions

Memory Verse

Impressions

"Humility is something we should constantly pray for, yet never thank God that we have."
- Martin DeHaan

My Words to God

Date:_____

Gratitude & Praise

_____

_____

_____

_____

Prayer for Others

_____

_____

_____

_____

Prayers for Self

_____

_____

_____

_____

_____

God's Word to Me

Reflections from Bible Time/Devotions

....

....

....

....

....

Memory Verse

....

....

....

Impressions

....

....

....

....

*"Every tomorrow has two handles. We can take hold of it
with the handle of anxiety or the handle of faith"*
- Henry Ward Beecher

My Words to God

Date:_____

Gratitude & Praise

What fills your heart with gratitude & praise?

Prayer for Others

Lift the names, and hearts

Prayers for Self

Let your prayers draw honour to Christ for righteousness

Tell God what's on your heart at night

God's Word to Me

Reflections from Bible Time/Devotions

_____
_____
_____
_____
_____

Memory Verse

_____
_____
_____

Impressions

_____
_____
_____
_____

"Trust in the Lord with all your heart and lean not on your
own understanding"
- Proverbs 3:5

My Words to God

Date:_____

Gratitude & Praise

_____

_____

_____

_____

Prayer for Others

_____

_____

_____

_____

Prayers for Self

_____

_____

_____

_____

God's Word to Me

Reflections from Bible Time/Devotions

....

....

....

....

....

Memory Verse

....

....

....

Impressions

....

....

....

....

"We must remember that the shortest distance between our problems
and their solutions is the distance between our knees and the floor"
- Charles Stanley

My Words to God

Date:_____

Gratitude & Praise

What filled your heart and how can it be praised?

Prayer for Others

Lift up those around you.

Prayers for Self

_Lay our your heart. Ask God for if there be righteousness.
Tell God what is on your heart and mind._

God's Word to Me

Reflections from Bible Time/Devotions

_____

_____

_____

_____

_____

Memory Verse

_____

_____

_____

Impressions

_____

_____

_____

_____

"God never said that the journey would be easy, but He did
say that the arrival would be worthwhile."
- Max Lucado

My Words to God

Date:_____

Gratitude & Praise

What lifted your heart...the reason to be praise?

Prayer for Others

Lift the people around you.

Prayers for Self

Let your prayers should cause it this at the Father...nothing.
Tell God what's on your mind is mind.

God's Word to Me

Reflections from Bible Time/Devotions

....

....

....

....

....

Memory Verse

....

....

....

Impressions

....

....

....

....

"Whoever does not love does not know God, because God is love"
- 1 John 4:8

My Words to God

Date:_____

Gratitude & Praise

....

....

....

....

Prayer for Others

....

....

....

....

Prayers for Self

....

....

....

....

....

God's Word to Me

Reflections from Bible Time/Devotions

....

....

....

....

....

Memory Verse

....

....

....

Impressions

....

....

....

....

"God does not give us everything we want, but He does fulfill His promises, leading us along the best and straightest paths to Himself."
- Dietrich Bonhoeffer

My Words to God

Gratitude & Praise

What fills your heart with gratitude & praise?

....

....

....

....

Prayer for Others

Who in your life needs prayer?

....

....

....

....

Prayers for Self

Let your worries ebbing homage to God as they flow into ebbing steady to God. What is God's whisper in your heart & mind?

....

....

....

....

God's Word to Me

Reflections from Bible Time/Devotions

Memory Verse

Impressions

"It is not the trials in your life that develop or destroy you, but
rather your response to those hardships"
- Charles Stanley

My Words to God

Date:_____

Gratitude & Praise

Prayer for Others

Prayers for Self

God's Word to Me

Reflections from Bible Time/Devotions

....

....

....

....

....

Memory Verse

....

....

....

Impressions

....

....

....

....

"If you believe in a God who controls the big things, you have to believe in a God who controls the little things. It is we, of course, to whom things look 'little' or 'big.'"
- Elisabeth Elliot

My Words to God

Date:_____

Gratitude & Praise

....

....

....

....

Prayer for Others

....

....

....

....

Prayers for Self

....

....

....

....

God's Word to Me

Reflections from Bible Time/Devotions

Memory Verse

Impressions

"The greater your knowledge of the goodness and grace of God on your life, the more likely you are to praise Him in the storm"
- Matt Chandler

My Words to God

Date:_____

Gratitude & Praise

Prayer for Others

Prayers for Self

God's Word to Me

Reflections from Bible Time/Devotions

Memory Verse

Impressions

"Be devoted to one another in love. Honor one another above yourselves."
- Romans 12:10

My Words to God

Date:_____

Gratitude & Praise

What Blessings have I experienced from God?

Prayer for Others

Lift up those in need...

Prayers for Self

Let your requests flow unceasingly before the Lord in prayer.
Let God know what's on your heart & mind.

God's Word to Me

Reflections from Bible Time/Devotions

Memory Verse

Impressions

"God is most glorified in us when we are most satisfied in Him."
- John Piper

My Words to God

Date:_____

Gratitude & Praise

_____

_____

_____

_____

Prayer for Others

_____

_____

_____

_____

Prayers for Self

_____

_____

_____

_____

God's Word to Me

Reflections from Bible Time/Devotions

Memory Verse

Impressions

"To be a Christian means to forgive the inexcusable, because
God has forgiven the inexcusable in you"
- C.S. Lewis

My Words to God

Date:_____

Gratitude & Praise

....

....

....

....

Prayer for Others

....

....

....

....

Prayers for Self

....

....

....

....

God's Word to Me

Reflections from Bible Time/Devotions

Memory Verse

Impressions

"You thought you were being made into a decent little cottage but He is building a palace. He intends to come and live in it Himself"
— C.S. Lewis

My Words to God

Date:_____

Gratitude & Praise

....

....

....

....

Prayer for Others

....

....

....

....

Prayers for Self

....

....

....

....

God's Word to Me

Reflections from Bible Time/Devotions

Memory Verse

Impressions

"If you are forgetful of the Lord, you will not pray, and without prayer the soul will
not dwell in the love of God, for the grace of the Holy Spirit comes through prayer"
- Elizabeth P. Fitzgerald

My Words to God

Date:_____

<u>Gratitude & Praise</u>

<u>Prayer for Others</u>

<u>Prayers for Self</u>

God's Word to Me

Reflections from Bible Time/Devotions

_____

Memory Verse

_____

Impressions

_____

"When I consider the cross of Christ, how can anything that
I do be called a sacrifice?"
- Amy Carmichael

My Words to God

Date:_____

Gratitude & Praise

....

....

....

....

Prayer for Others

....

....

....

....

Prayers for Self

....

....

....

....

God's Word to Me

Reflections from Bible Time/Devotions

....

....

....

....

....

Memory Verse

....

....

....

Impressions

....

....

....

....

"God's love is felt the most when you realize the gravity
of your sins"
- Janneker Lawrence Daniel

My Words to God

Date:_____

Gratitude & Praise

....

....

....

....

Prayer for Others

....

....

....

....

Prayers for Self

....

....

....

....

....

God's Word to Me

Reflections from Bible Time/Devotions

....

....

....

....

....

Memory Verse

....

....

....

Impressions

....

....

....

....

"Then Jesus said, "Did I not tell you that if you believe, you
will see the glory of God?"
- John 11:40

My Words to God

Date:_____

Gratitude & Praise

_____

_____

_____

_____

Prayer for Others

_____

_____

_____

_____

Prayers for Self

_____

_____

_____

_____

God's Word to Me

Reflections from Bible Time/Devotions

Memory Verse

Impressions

"The quicker we realize that both the 0.50¢ and the $50 million really belong to God
and that He has entrusted them to our care only for His glory and purpose,
is the quicker we will be able to have equal gratitude for them both"
- Shane Dennis

My Words to God

Date:_____

Gratitude & Praise

What filled your heart with gratitude to praise?

Prayer for Others

Names, issues and needs

Prayers for Self

Let your prayers show humility. Adjust for righteousness.
Ask God What's on your mind at man't

God's Word to Me

Reflections from Bible Time/Devotions

Memory Verse

Impressions

"If you are forgetful of the Lord, you will not pray, and without prayer the soul will not dwell in the love of God, for the grace of the Holy Spirit comes through prayer"
- Elizabeth P. Fitzgerald

My Words to God

Date:_____

Gratitude & Praise

Prayer for Others

Prayers for Self

God's Word to Me

Reflections from Bible Time/Devotions

....

....

....

....

....

Memory Verse

....

....

....

Impressions

....

....

....

....

"We have to pray with our eyes on God, not on the difficulties."
- Oswald Chambers

My Words to God

Date:_____

Gratitude & Praise

_____

_____

_____

_____

Prayer for Others

_____

_____

_____

_____

Prayers for Self

_____

_____

_____

_____

God's Word to Me

Reflections from Bible Time/Devotions

_____

_____

_____

_____

Memory Verse

_____

_____

_____

Impressions

_____

_____

_____

"One of the Devil's great lies is that the path to a fulfilling life
is to live for one's self"
- Andrew B. Ray

My Words to God

Date:_____

Gratitude & Praise

What filled your heart with gratitude & praise?

Prayer for Others

Intercede for those you love as

Prayers for Self

Let your prayers show humble & thirst for righteousness
that God hears as your heart is joyful

God's Word to Me

Reflections from Bible Time/Devotions

....

....

....

....

....

Memory Verse

....

....

....

Impressions

....

....

....

....

"Basically, there are two paths you can walk: faith or fear. It's impossible to simultaneously trust God and not trust God"
- Charles Stanley

My Words to God

Date:_____

Gratitude & Praise

_____

_____

_____

_____

Prayer for Others

_____

_____

_____

_____

Prayers for Self

_____

_____

_____

_____

_____

God's Word to Me

Reflections from Bible Time/Devotions

Memory Verse

Impressions

"Life is God's novel. Let him write it"
- Isaac Bashevis Singer

My Words to God

Date:_____

Gratitude & Praise

_____

_____

_____

_____

Prayer for Others

_____

_____

_____

_____

Prayers for Self

_____

_____

_____

_____

God's Word to Me

Reflections from Bible Time/Devotions

....

....

....

....

....

Memory Verse

....

....

....

Impressions

....

....

....

....

"Worry does not empty tomorrow of its sorrows, it empties
today of its strength"
- Corrie Ten Boom

My Words to God

Date:_____

Gratitude & Praise

....

....

....

....

Prayer for Others

....

....

....

....

Prayers for Self

....

....

....

....

God's Word to Me

Reflections from Bible Time/Devotions

....

....

....

....

....

Memory Verse

....

....

....

Impressions

....

....

....

"Do not be anxious about anything, but in everything, by prayer and petition, with thanksgiving, present your requests to God"
- Philippians 4:6-7

My Words to God

Date:_____

Gratitude & Praise

(faint prompt text)

Prayer for Others

(faint prompt text)

Prayers for Self

(faint prompt text)

God's Word to Me

Reflections from Bible Time/Devotions

Memory Verse

Impressions

"Sir, my concern is not whether God is on our side; my greatest
concern is to be on God's side, for God is always right"
- Abraham Lincoln

My Words to God

Date:_____

Gratitude & Praise

_____

_____

_____

_____

Prayer for Others

_____

_____

_____

_____

Prayers for Self

_____

_____

_____

_____

God's Word to Me

Reflections from Bible Time/Devotions

....

....

....

....

....

Memory Verse

....

....

....

Impressions

....

....

....

....

"God never made a promise that was too good to be true"
- Dwight L. Moody

My Words to God

Date:_____

Gratitude & Praise

What fills your heart with gratitude? or joy?
....

....

....

....

Prayer for Others

Who do you want to pray for?
....

....

....

....

Prayers for Self

Let your prayers place before God your heart's intentions.
What do you ask of you in your mind & spirit?
....

....

....

....

God's Word to Me

Reflections from Bible Time/Devotions

....

....

....

....

....

Memory Verse

....

....

....

Impressions

....

....

....

"The Christian shoemaker does his duty not by putting little crosses on the shoes,
but by making good shoes, because God is interested in good craftsmanship"
- Martin Luther

My Words to God

Date:_____

Gratitude & Praise

_____

_____

_____

_____

Prayer for Others

_____

_____

_____

_____

Prayers for Self

_____

_____

_____

_____

God's Word to Me

Reflections from Bible Time/Devotions

Memory Verse

Impressions

"Earn as much as you can. Save as much as you can. Invest
as much as you can. Give as much as you can."
- John Wesley

My Words to God

Date:_____

Gratitude & Praise

Prayer for Others

Prayers for Self

God's Word to Me

Reflections from Bible Time/Devotions

Memory Verse

Impressions

"I'm not perfect. I'm never going to be. And that's the great thing about
living the Christian life and trying to live by faith, is you're trying
to get better every day. You're trying to improve"
- Tim Tebow

My Words to God

Date:_____

Gratitude & Praise

Prayer for Others

Prayers for Self

God's Word to Me

Reflections from Bible Time/Devotions

....

....

....

....

....

Memory Verse

....

....

....

Impressions

....

....

....

....

"If the Holy Spirit guides us, He will do it according to the
Scriptures and never contrary to them"
- George Muller

My Words to God

Date:_____

Gratitude & Praise

What filled your heart with gratitude & praise?

Prayer for Others

Lord, list people that need...

Prayers for Self

Let your prayers spontaneous to this important prayer.
Tell God What's on your heart & mind.

God's Word to Me

Reflections from Bible Time/Devotions

Memory Verse

Impressions

"Remember who you are. Don't compromise for anyone, for any reason. You are a child of the Almighty God. Live that truth."
- Lysa Terkeurst

My Words to God

Date:_____

Gratitude & Praise

_____

_____

_____

_____

Prayer for Others

_____

_____

_____

_____

Prayers for Self

_____

_____

_____

_____

God's Word to Me

Reflections from Bible Time/Devotions

Memory Verse

Impressions

"Where God guides, He provides"
- Isaiah 58:11

My Words to God

Date:_____

Gratitude & Praise

_____

_____

_____

Prayer for Others

_____

_____

_____

Prayers for Self

_____

_____

_____

_____

God's Word to Me

Reflections from Bible Time/Devotions

Memory Verse

Impressions

"Christ literally walked in our shoes"
- Tim Keller

My Words to God

Date:_____

Gratitude & Praise

....

....

....

....

Prayer for Others

....

....

....

....

Prayers for Self

....

....

....

....

God's Word to Me

Reflections from Bible Time/Devotions

Memory Verse

Impressions

"Everything is possible for one who believes"
- Mark 9:23

My Words to God

Date:_____

Gratitude & Praise

_____

_____

_____

_____

Prayer for Others

_____

_____

_____

_____

Prayers for Self

_____

_____

_____

_____

God's Word to Me

Reflections from Bible Time/Devotions

Memory Verse

Impressions

"The will of God will not take us where the grace of God
cannot sustain us"
- Billy Graham

My Words to God

Date:_____

Gratitude & Praise

When filled your heart with gratitude & praise?

Prayer for Others

Lift the needs of your loved ones to

Prayers for Self

Let your prayers show hunger & thirst for righteousness

Tell God what's on your heart & mind

God's Word to Me

Reflections from Bible Time/Devotions

_____

_____

_____

_____

Memory Verse

_____

_____

Impressions

_____

_____

_____

_____

"Be faithful in small things because it is in them that your strength lies"
- Mother Teresa

My Words to God

Date:_____

Gratitude & Praise

What filled your heart with gratitude & praise?

Prayer for Others

List the names and needs.

Prayers for Self

Let your prayers show to pour of christ for christ conscious.
Tell God what's on your heart & mind.

God's Word to Me

Reflections from Bible Time/Devotions

Memory Verse

Impressions

"He is no fool who gives what he cannot keep, to gain what he cannot lose."
- Jim Elliot

My Words to God

Date:_____

Gratitude & Praise

_____

_____

_____

_____

Prayer for Others

_____

_____

_____

_____

Prayers for Self

_____

_____

_____

_____

God's Word to Me

Reflections from Bible Time/Devotions

Memory Verse

Impressions

"Our greatest fear should not be of failure but of succeeding at things in life that don't really matter"
- Francis Chan

My Words to God

Date:_____

Gratitude & Praise

....

....

....

....

Prayer for Others

....

....

....

....

Prayers for Self

....

....

....

....

God's Word to Me

Reflections from Bible Time/Devotions

Memory Verse

Impressions

"He who lays up treasures on earth spends his life backing away from his treasures. To him, death is loss. He who lays up treasures in heaven looks forward to eternity; he's moving daily toward his treasures. To him, death is gain"
- Randy Alcorn

My Words to God

Date:_____

Gratitude & Praise

_____

_____

_____

_____

Prayer for Others

_____

_____

_____

_____

Prayers for Self

_____

_____

_____

_____

_____

God's Word to Me

Reflections from Bible Time/Devotions

Memory Verse

Impressions

"God is able to take the mess of our past and turn it into a message.
He takes the trials and tests and turns them into a testimony."
- Christine Caine

My Words to God

Date:_____

Gratitude & Praise

_____

_____

_____

_____

Prayer for Others

_____

_____

_____

_____

Prayers for Self

_____

_____

_____

_____

God's Word to Me

Reflections from Bible Time/Devotions

....

....

....

....

....

Memory Verse

....

....

....

Impressions

....

....

....

....

"God loves each of us as if there were only one of us"
- Augustine

My Words to God

Date:_____

Gratitude & Praise

Prayer for Others

Prayers for Self

God's Word to Me

Reflections from Bible Time/Devotions

Memory Verse

Impressions

"The best and most beautiful things in this world cannot
be seen or even heard, but must be felt with the heart."
- Helen Keller

My Words to God

Date:_____

Gratitude & Praise

Write filled your heart with gratitude & praise?

Prayer for Others

Are the names of others?

Prayers for Self

Let your prayers show people a blessing and encourage.
Let God speak on your heart & mind.

God's Word to Me

Reflections from Bible Time/Devotions

Memory Verse

Impressions

"If God is your partner, make your plans BIG!"
- D.L. Moody

My Words to God

Date:_____

Gratitude & Praise

What/Who are you grateful for? What/Who do you praise?

Prayer for Others

Lift up people in your life.

Prayers for Self

Let your requests flow! Confess to Him & ask forgiveness.
Tell God What's on your heart & mind.

God's Word to Me

<u>Reflections from Bible Time/Devotions</u>

<u>Memory Verse</u>

<u>Impressions</u>

"As iron sharpens iron, so one person sharpens another"
- Proverbs 27:17

My Words to God

Date:_____

Gratitude & Praise

Prayer for Others

Prayers for Self

God's Word to Me

Reflections from Bible Time/Devotions

Memory Verse

Impressions

"The only thing necessary for the triumph of evil is for
good men to do nothing."
- Edmund Burke

My Words to God

Date:_____

Gratitude & Praise

What fills your heart with thanks & praise?

Prayer for Others

Lift up your children.

Prayers for Self

Let your praises flow to your Father for righteousness.

Tell God what's on your heart & mind.

God's Word to Me

Reflections from Bible Time/Devotions

....
....
....
....
....

Memory Verse

....
....
....

Impressions

....
....
....
....

"God's work done in God's way will never lack God's supplies"
- Hudson Taylor

My Words to God

Date:_____

Gratitude & Praise

Prayer for Others

Prayers for Self

God's Word to Me

Reflections from Bible Time/Devotions

Memory Verse

Impressions

"My faith didn't remove the pain, but it got me through the pain. Trusting God didn't diminish or vanquish the anguish, but it enabled me to endure it"
- Robert Rogers

My Words to God

Date:_____

Gratitude & Praise

....

....

....

....

Prayer for Others

....

....

....

....

Prayers for Self

....

....

....

....

God's Word to Me

Reflections from Bible Time/Devotions

Memory Verse

Impressions

"Every single thing He has ever or will ever say is true. The simplicity of faith is this: taking God's Word for it"
- Jackie Hill Perry

My Words to God

Date:_____

Gratitude & Praise

Prayer for Others

Prayers for Self

God's Word to Me

Reflections from Bible Time/Devotions

....

....

....

....

....

Memory Verse

....

....

....

Impressions

....

....

....

....

"Faith is taking the first step even when you don't see the whole staircase"
- Martin Luther King, Jr.

My Words to God

Date:_____

Gratitude & Praise

What fills your heart with gratitude & praise?

Prayer for Others

Who needs your prayers?

Prayers for Self

Let your prayers show hunger & thirst for righteousness.
Tell God what's on your heart & mind.

God's Word to Me

Reflections from Bible Time/Devotions

....

....

....

....

....

Memory Verse

....

....

....

Impressions

....

....

....

....

"If you are too busy to pray, you are busier than God wants you to be"
- Wanda E. Brunstetter

My Words to God

Date:_____

Gratitude & Praise

....

....

....

....

Prayer for Others

....

....

....

....

Prayers for Self

....

....

....

....

....

God's Word to Me

Reflections from Bible Time/Devotions

Memory Verse

Impressions

"He said "Love...as I have loved you." We cannot love too much"
- Amy Carmichael

My Words to God

Date:_____

Gratitude & Praise

Prayer for Others

Prayers for Self

God's Word to Me

Reflections from Bible Time/Devotions

_____

_____

_____

_____

_____

Memory Verse

_____

_____

_____

Impressions

_____

_____

_____

_____

"Unconditional love is an illogical notion, but such a great
and powerful one"
- A.J. Jacobs

My Words to God

Date:_____

Gratitude & Praise

What filled your heart with gratitude & praise?

Prayer for Others

Lift their names and needs

Prayers for Self

Let your heart's cries be heard. Share your worries, hopes, and needs with God. What is on your heart to write?

God's Word to Me

Reflections from Bible Time/Devotions

_____

_____

_____

_____

Memory Verse

_____

_____

Impressions

_____

_____

_____

"Focus on giants - you stumble. Focus on God - Giants tumble"
- Max Lucado

My Words to God

Date:_____

Gratitude & Praise

....

....

....

....

Prayer for Others

....

....

....

....

Prayers for Self

....

....

....

....

God's Word to Me

<u>Reflections from Bible Time/Devotions</u>

<u>Memory Verse</u>

<u>Impressions</u>

"Be kind and compassionate to one another, forgiving each
other, just as in Christ God forgave you"
- Ephesians 4:32

My Words to God

Date:_____

Gratitude & Praise

Pour out your heart with gratitude & praise?

Prayer for Others

Lord, there are others who need...

Prayers for Self

Let your prayers show hunger & thirst for righteousness?
Tell God what's on your heart & mind.

God's Word to Me

Reflections from Bible Time/Devotions

....

....

....

....

....

Memory Verse

....

....

....

Impressions

....

....

....

....

"Be not forgetful to entertain strangers; for thereby some
have entertained angels unawares"
- Serena B. Miller

My Words to God

Date:_____

Gratitude & Praise

_____

_____

_____

_____

Prayer for Others

_____

_____

_____

_____

Prayers for Self

_____

_____

_____

_____

God's Word to Me

Reflections from Bible Time/Devotions

....

....

....

....

....

Memory Verse

....

....

....

Impressions

....

....

....

....

"Do all the good you can, By all the means you can, In all the ways you can, In all the places you can, At all the times you can, To all the people you can, As long as ever you can"
- John Wesley

My Words to God

Date:_____

Gratitude & Praise

....

....

....

....

Prayer for Others

....

....

....

....

Prayers for Self

....

....

....

....

God's Word to Me

Reflections from Bible Time/Devotions

Memory Verse

Impressions

"Faith does not eliminate questions. But faith knows where
to take them"
- Elisabeth Elliot

My Words to God

Date:_____

Gratitude & Praise

_____

_____

_____

_____

Prayer for Others

_____

_____

_____

_____

Prayers for Self

_____

_____

_____

_____

_____

God's Word to Me

Reflections from Bible Time/Devotions

Memory Verse

Impressions

"We may speak about a place where there are no tears, no death, no fear, no night; but those are just the benefits of heaven. The beauty of heaven is seeing God"
- Max Lucado

My Words to God

Date:_____

Gratitude & Praise

_____

_____

_____

_____

Prayer for Others

_____

_____

_____

_____

Prayers for Self

_____

_____

_____

_____

God's Word to Me

Reflections from Bible Time/Devotions

Memory Verse

Impressions

"As long as you do things for God, you are a Hall of Famer
in heaven's list"
- Rick Warren

My Words to God

Date:_____

Gratitude & Praise

_____

_____

_____

_____

Prayer for Others

_____

_____

_____

_____

Prayers for Self

_____

_____

_____

_____

God's Word to Me

Reflections from Bible Time/Devotions

Memory Verse

Impressions

"We never grow closer to God when we just live life. It takes
deliberate pursuit and attentiveness"
- Francis Chan

My Words to God

Date:_____

Gratitude & Praise

Prayer for Others

Prayers for Self

God's Word to Me

Reflections from Bible Time/Devotions

Memory Verse

Impressions

"Worry about tomorrow steals the joy from today"
- Barbara Cameron

My Words to God

Date:_____

Gratitude & Praise

Prayer for Others

Prayers for Self

God's Word to Me

Reflections from Bible Time/Devotions

Memory Verse

Impressions

"God wants the whole person and He will not rest till He
gets us in entirety. No part of the man will do."
- A.W. Tozer

My Words to God

Date:_____

Gratitude & Praise

What fills my heart with gratitude & praise?

Prayer for Others

Intercession and needs

Prayers for Self

Let your desires show hunger & thirst for righteousness
Tell God what's on your heart & mind

God's Word to Me

<u>Reflections from Bible Time/Devotions</u>

<u>Memory Verse</u>

<u>Impressions</u>

"We fear men so much, because we fear God so little"
- William Gurnall

My Words to God

Date:_____

Gratitude & Praise

_____

_____

_____

Prayer for Others

_____

_____

_____

Prayers for Self

_____

_____

_____

_____

God's Word to Me

Reflections from Bible Time/Devotions

Memory Verse

Impressions

"Put on the full armor of God, so that you can take your
stand against the devil's schemes"
- Ephesians 6:11

My Words to God

Date:_____

Gratitude & Praise

What filled your heart with gratitude & praise?

Prayer for Others

Here is a prayer for others

Prayers for Self

Lay your own personal requests & things for which you need help.
Tell God what's on your heart & mind.

You did it! You stuck with it.

Prayer For You

Lord, I pray for my awesome friend who just completed this journal.
Please grant them your peace, love, grace and favour.
Please protect them from the evils of this world.
I pray that you will guide their paths and help them to make decisions that honour You always.

Give them wisdom, courage, strength and endurance to fight the good fight of faith.
In Jesus' name, Amen!

Blessings my friend, I love you.